Shiver me timbers!
Discovery in Antarctica, 1901

Written by Jill Sim
Illustrated by Andy Sim

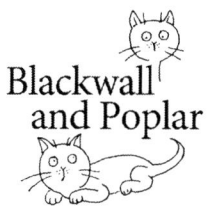

Blackwall
and Poplar

Published by Blackwall and Poplar

Copyright © 2016 Jill Sim and Andy Sim

All rights reserved. No part of this book may be reproduced in any form or by any electronic or mechanical means including storage and retrieval systems without permission in writing from the copyright holders.

The moral right of the author has been asserted.

ISBN: 978-1-5262-0284-0

Thanks to Imogen for all the help.

Many of the illustrations in this book are based on drawings and photographs made by the crew of the 1901 British Antarctic Expedition. The Discovery's present home at Discovery Point in Dundee is an award-winning five-star visitor attraction which tells the stories of the ship's many voyages. This book tells the first.

blackwallandpoplar.com

To young explorers everywhere.

Ahoy there!

Ahoy there!
I am the Royal Research Ship Discovery and this is my story. You can find me these days on the waterfront in Dundee. I live in a little dock built especially for me, next to a museum called Discovery Point. But I haven't always lived here…

I have been all over the world, but I'm most famous for going South to the Antarctic with the explorer Captain Robert Falcon Scott.

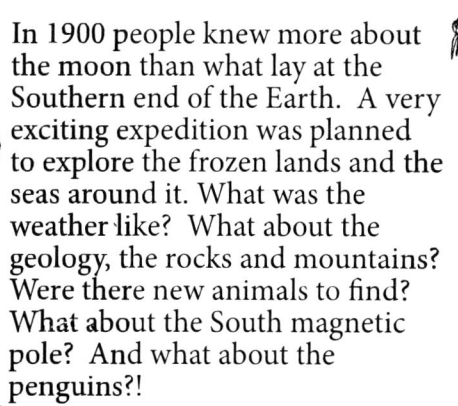

In 1900 people knew more about the moon than what lay at the Southern end of the Earth. A very exciting expedition was planned to explore the frozen lands and the seas around it. What was the weather like? What about the geology, the rocks and mountains? Were there new animals to find? What about the South magnetic pole? And what about the penguins?!

Me Timbers

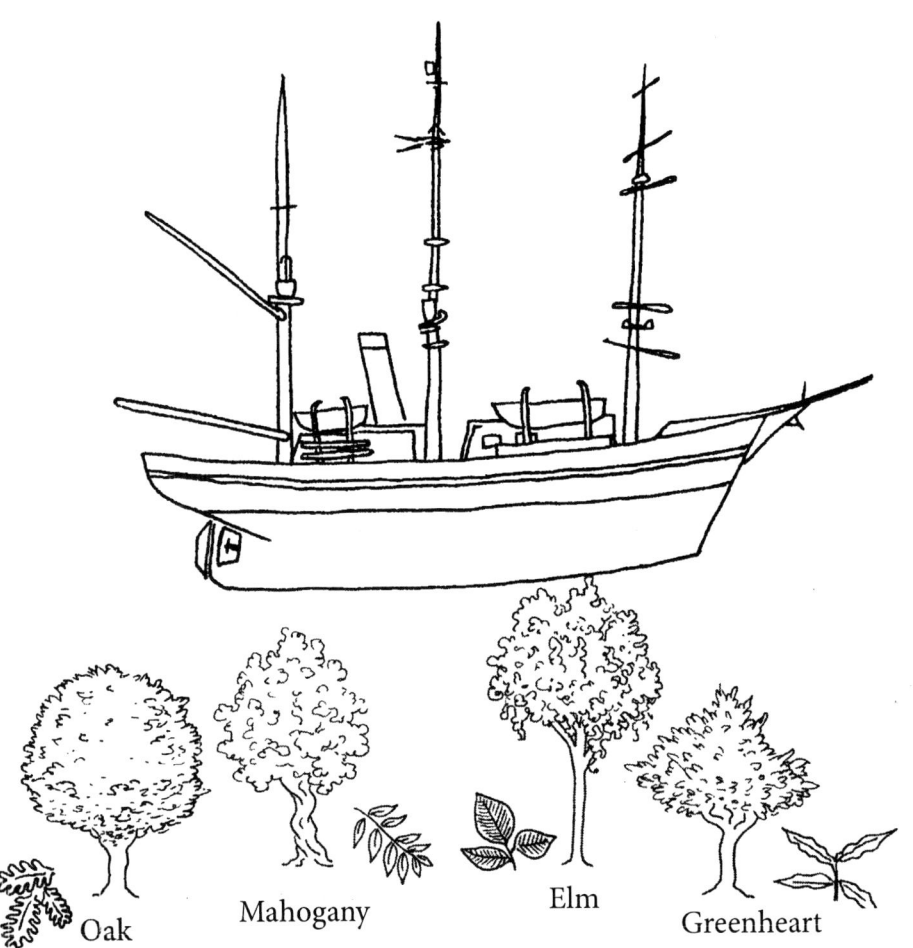

Over one hundred years ago, in the year 1900 my timbers were shaped by the shipbuilding carpenters of Dundee. Hundreds of men worked in the dockyards hammering, sawing, chiselling and drilling until they had turned trees into me!

My timbers come from all over the world. Mahogany from Honduras, Greenheart from Guyana, Oak and Elm from England and pine from Riga in Latvia. My strongest wood is on the outside of my hull. It's called Greenheart - even though it's painted black!

At the front I am strengthened with metal plates, bent round to make a sharp, slicing bow. I was built specially for scientific research in Antarctica, so I had to be much stronger than the steel ships that were being built in most ship yards. I would have to be a proper ice-breaker, to bash through frozen seas, and back then metal ships weren't so strong.....I expect you know what happened to the poor old Titanic!

I have three masts that were made of Oregon pine (today they are made of Scots pine) and I held fifteen large canvas sails.

My spinning propeller, and my steering rudder, can both be lifted up onto the deck to protect them from the ice, or to repair them out of the water.

You can't come peeking into portholes along my sides. I don't have any, because they would have weakened my hull. Instead I have raised windows on my deck. The sailors called these 'ankle bashers' because they kept tripping over them! Woops!

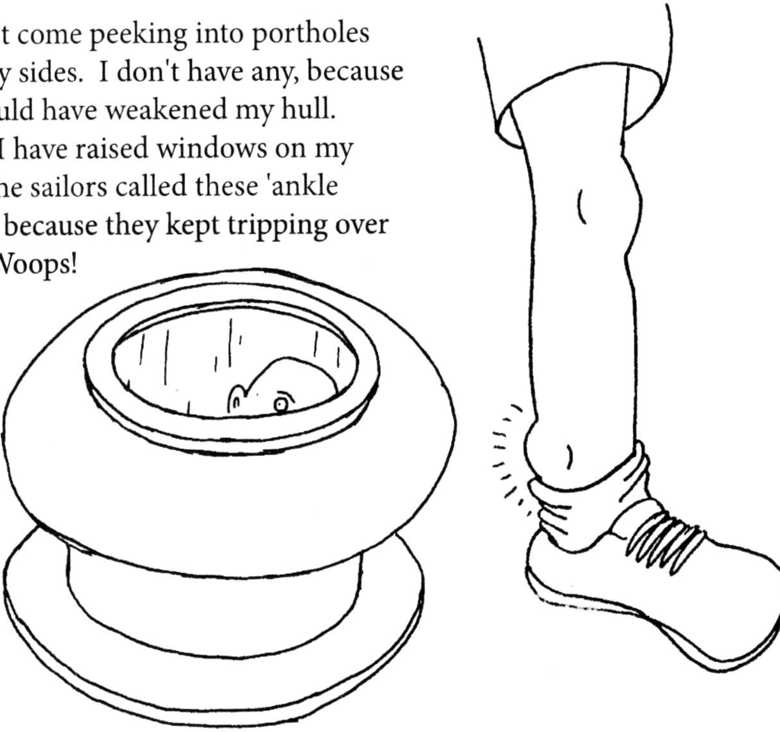

Launch time!

It took less than a year for me to be completed. Quick work! I felt very proud with my three sturdy masts, my new sails and ropes; and my very special steam engine, all made in Dundee. That's right, I'm a sailing ship AND a steam ship! On 21st March 1901, Lady Markham smashed a bottle of wine over my bow and I slid into the river Tay. I'd have preferred a bottle of Irn Bru, but it's tradition to send ships off with alcohol. I was the strongest ship ever built, no wonder everyone cheered so loudly!

I meet the Captain

When Commander Robert Falcon Scott and his crew, (and his little Scottish terrier, Scamp) came aboard I began to learn about my first trip and what would be expected of me. Our voyage was called the British National Antarctic Expedition. It sounded very important.

To be honest I was a little bit nervous, because it was clear that we were going to the other end of the world to places where very few people had been before. The Royal Geographic Society wanted Britain to be first to find out what lay in the frozen land to the south. I knew it would be very cold, but I hadn't realised that the sea would freeze right round me and that I'd be stuck fast in the ice! But, even though I was worried, I couldn't wait for the adventure to begin.

Supplies, supplies

I didn't have to wait very long. Pretty soon my strong timbers were being filled with all manner of things. Coal for the engines, three years' worth of food for the men, spare ropes, tools, canvas and timber, sledges, dog food for the huskies (they came aboard later), skis, tents, sleeping bags, boats, huts, warm clothes, medicines, microscopes and other scientific equipment, cameras, paints, hundreds of books, a windmill to make electricity and much more.   There was even a hot air balloon! Blackwall and Poplar were the two brave kittens who came aboard in London and who soon made themselves at home on the mess deck. The mess deck on a ship is where the men live and eat. If they make a mess, they have to clean it up!

And we're off!

We stopped at Cowes on the Isle of Wight and I was very surprised when King Edward VII and Queen Alexandra came aboard to wish us goodbye, good luck and God speed. The Queen's little Pekingese dog got scared and jumped into the sea and one of the sailors had to jump in to rescue it! The royals left with their soggy doggy and pretty soon Captain Scott announced that it was time for us to go. With the wind filling my sails, I settled into the water and felt very proud and important as I sped along.

There were 49 men on board when we left Britain on 6th August 1901. We didn't know it then, but many of them would return to Antarctica on other expeditions. Captain Scott and Sir Ernest Shackleton are two of the most famous names in polar history and I'm very proud that they first went south to Antarctica with me!

The crew were very excited and happy as we sailed away and even though my timbers leaked a little, they said I was the finest three masted barque ever.

Our first stop was in Funchal on the island of Madeira, but not for long, as Captain Scott was keen to get south as soon as possible. We needed to arrive in Antarctica in the summer time so that the sea would not yet be frozen solid! In the south it's opposite to the Northern Hemisphere - December or January would be best for us.

Rock and roll!

We got to Cape Town in South Africa on 3rd October 1901 and my bunkers were refilled with coal. We ran into a lot of stormy weather after this and I have to admit I did roll around a lot in the water.
This made life difficult for everyone on board, but Captain Scott and Mr Skelton the engineer were still very pleased with me and how I coped with the gales and heavy seas.

In the kitchen the cook had rails around the stove to stop the pots from slipping off, and in the mess rooms tables had 'fiddle rails' to catch the plates. Even so, sometimes when I rolled over on a big wave the men ended up wearing their dinner!

The books would fall off the shelves, the chairs and the piano would fall over with a crash and everything would tumble about in the cargo hold. Ernest Shackleton was in charge of storing everything correctly and I'm afraid I caused him a lot of work.

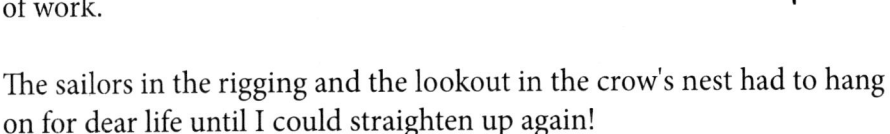

The sailors in the rigging and the lookout in the crow's nest had to hang on for dear life until I could straighten up again!

My first ice

On the 15th November 1901 I saw ice for the first time. That night I was surrounded by pack ice. Pack ice is up to a metre thick and floats in small pieces on the freezing sea. I had to scrape and push through it all night. Two days later I had to stop. All we could see was solid white ice for miles in front. It certainly made my timbers shiver, but I wasn't worried! My sides are 66cm thick, this is what I'm made for! But, Captain Scott gave the order to leave and head for New Zealand where we would stock up on food and coal. I went to dry dock and they tried very hard to find my leaks, but the complicated way all the different wood in my hull is constructed made this an almost impossible task.

In New Zealand

Everyone in New Zealand seemed to be very excited and enthusiastic about our expedition and many people came to admire me in Lyttleton Harbour. I was always a bit of a celebrity! Captain Scott found a new home for Scamp, having decided that Antarctica was too risky for the little dog.

But we had 23 new dogs on board now! Huskies from Siberia who were to pull the sledges across the ice on the expeditions. Even more of a surprise to me were the 45 sheep given as a gift from the farmers of New Zealand. They would take care of Sunday dinner for a while!

Sad Farewells

At 2 o'clock on 21st December 1901 I steamed out of the harbour feeling very proud, as bands played and thousands of people waved and cheered. Many had come on special trains from Christchurch, just to wish us good luck and see me set sail! I gave them a blast on my steam whistle and headed south.

Suddenly our happy mood turned to anguish. A young seaman called Charles Bonner was high above in my crow's nest, waving goodbye to the crowds. He had been sitting on the truck at the top of the mast when he jumped up to give a last wave. He grabbed my little windvane, but it snapped and he fell head first onto the deck! He died instantly. Poor lad! Everyone felt so sad and shocked to lose one of our most popular young sailors. We stopped in Port Chalmers a few kilometres along the coast for his funeral. While here, Tom Crean, a young Irish sailor volunteered to come along. Little did he realise it wouldn't be his only trip to Antarctica!

17

Feathered followers

On Christmas Eve we finally left New Zealand behind us and started on our exciting voyage of scientific research and discovery. The weather was fair so I made good progress without making anyone seasick. There are many birds in the Southern Ocean and they love to fly behind ships, so I often found I was being followed by petrels, fulmars, skua gulls and even enormous albatrosses.

Dr Edward Wilson was the ship's artist (and junior doctor) and he made the most amazing sketches and paintings of them. The crew caught specimens of each bird to bring back to the natural history museums in Britain.

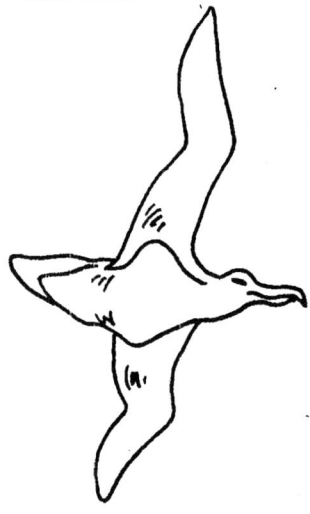

Antarctica at last!

On 2nd January 1902 things went very quiet as I found myself surrounded by thick icy fog, I slowed down so that everyone could keep a sharp lookout. After some hours the grey mist cleared and we saw our very first iceberg. It was a massively huge block of ice floating silently along, with a flat top and much more ice under the water than above! In the Antarctic summer daylight lasts for 24 hours a day. The iceberg looked beautiful, but eerily dangerous in this light. I felt my timbers shiver once again.

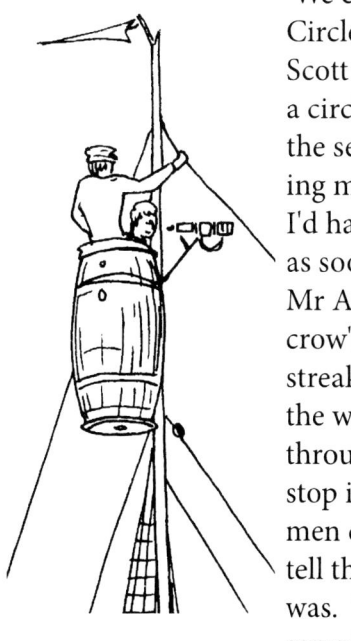

We crossed the Antarctic Circle the next day. Captain Scott said so, but I couldn't see a circle anywhere. I did notice the sea around me was growing more and more icy. I knew I'd have to get used to the cold as soon as possible! The Pilot, Mr Armitage stayed up in the crow's nest looking for black streaks of water that indicated the weakest ice for me to push through. Sometimes I would stop in an open pool so that the men could take soundings to tell them how deep the water was. They took water and ice samples and studied them with microscopes in the laboratory.

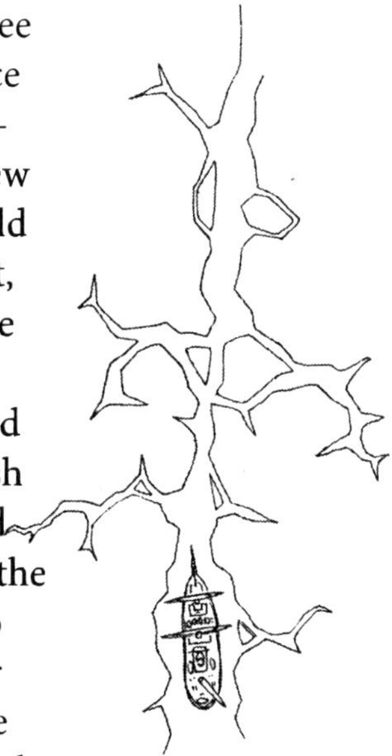

Antarctic animal life

Once among the ice we started to see the most wonderful of all Antarctic birds, - penguins! These cheerful little chaps would jump in and out of the water, swimming alongside me and sometimes they would just stare in amazement as I glided past. Some of the sailors could imitate their call and they would come running to see what all the fuss was about!

Lying on the ice and swimming in the water were different kinds of seals. The most common was the white seal, but there were also Ross seals, crab-eater seals, Weddell seals and leopard seals. Other sea animals the crew were studying included enormous whales, but also tiny plankton. On this expedition I brought back over 500 new species of animal life, never seen in Britain before. Science was very important to Captain Scott, his officers and men, so they were very proud and excited every time they made a new discovery. I often heard them pop a champagne cork in celebration!

Scurvy prevention

Sometimes we stopped to collect ice from a glacier. This was melted behind the stove in the galley so the men always had clear fresh water to drink.

At other times we stopped so the crew could practise skiing or have a game of football. They also hunted seals and penguins for food. I know this sounds cruel, but it was important that they eat fresh meat, not just the tinned corned beef and pheasant I was carrying for them. Fresh meat has more vitamin C and so stops people getting scurvy. Scurvy is a very painful disease that humans get when they have been at sea for too long and are not eating fresh food. Captain Scott knew this, so he insisted the cook serve up seal and penguin meat even though it didn't taste so good! Of course they also had the New Zealand mutton for Sundays. No freezer was needed, they just hung the meat in my rigging and it stayed perfectly frozen!

Back in the 1840s an explorer called Sir James Clark Ross had discovered volcanoes in Antarctica. He named them after his ships - Erebus and Terror. Now I saw them too, behind The Great Ice Barrier, as I steamed along. The officers saw that the sea ice had reduced in size since Ross had been there. This was the first sign of what we now call 'global warming', though we didn't know it at the time. There was so much snow that it was tricky to see what was frozen sea and what was land, but as soon as we clearly made out proper rocks, Captain Scott named the new land King Edward VII Land.

On several occasions we left messages in tins on poles painted red near the coast, so that ships coming next year could read our plans and perhaps come and find us! There was no other way of messaging, no phone, no radio, no wi-fi!

Going up

On 4th February 1902 Captain Scott became the first man to fly in a balloon over Antarctica. The balloon was filled with nitrogen and was named Eva. It was held to the ground by a rope which allowed him to rise safely 240 metres into the air. Ernest Shackleton went up next with a camera, but all that could be seen was mile after mile of white snow with white sky.

Doctor Wilson was very excited to see thousands of Emperor penguins through the telescope in the crow's nest, but the sea was beginning to freeze around my hull so there was no time to investigate. We had to find somewhere sheltered and safe to spend the winter.

My new home

Captain Scott chose a small ice filled bay at the top of McMurdo Sound on Ross Island. I put down my special ice anchors and the men tied me up. I began to feel the water freezing around me, chilling my timbers deeper and deeper, until I could feel my keel no longer. On 8th February 1902 I gave my last shiver, before being frozen solid in the ice. Although I felt the icy grip of Antarctica right around my hull, and I couldn't move at all, I still felt strong and safe.

By now I had gotten to know the men pretty well and they treated me with great care and respect. So, even though it was bitterly cold outside, I was warmed inside by the chatter, laughter and hustle and bustle of my friends the crew. I was moored by the mighty volcano Mount Erebus, which still active, sent clouds into the air from her warm heart.

The men set about building the huts I had carried. One became the Royal Terror Theatre where the sailors entertained each other with plays and concerts. Another was a magnetic observatory where the physicist Louis Bernacchi took regular readings on his magnetic instruments. An important part of the scientific research was to find out more about the south magnetic pole.

Captain Scott was keen to plan the exploration of the new land, to get farther south than any human had ever been before.
He sent a sledging party of eight men to leave a message further up the coast saying where I was frozen in, so that the relief ship next year would find me.
After a week some of the men returned in a blizzard of driving snow. The group had become lost and split up trying to find their friends in the dark. Seaman Vince had slipped and fallen over a cliff into the sea and Seaman Hare had disappeared.  A search party found their abandoned sledges and two of the dogs, but no sign of the two missing men. They came back with heavy hearts. The next morning I glimpsed a figure crawling down a hillside. The men working on the huts rushed off to find it was Hare. He was unharmed! He had fallen down exhausted in the snow whilst searching for his friends, fallen asleep and woken up 36 hours later under a blanket of snow! Sadly we all knew that poor George Vince must have drowned. A memorial cross was erected on the hillside, where it still stands today.

From April to August the sun stays
below the horizon, and winter comes to
Antarctica. It is far too cold and dark
to go exploring. This is the time for
planning and getting everything ready.
A sturdy canvas awning was erected
over my bridge and deck for shelter.
The windmill on my forecastle powered
electric lights, but the wind was too
strong and after a few months it was
broken beyond repair. After that it was
candles and oil lamps below.

Our first winter

The wardroom fires kept things as cosy as possible, but if the wind was in the wrong direction the smoke blew down into the ship, making the men yell and choke! Mind you they did a fair bit of smoking themselves on their pipes and cigarettes, so Dr Wilson opened the windows every morning to 'refresh the air below'.

The seamen had hammocks near the galley and they amused themselves with reading, card games, chess and a game called shove ha'penny. They were also busy sewing clothes, knitting socks and mittens, and writing letters. Letters they couldn't send for many months! Every morning they left me to collect ice for water. Then they had porridge with bread and butter, marmalade and jam for breakfast. They had their main meal of soup and seal or tinned meat followed by a jam or fruit tart (pie) at one o'clock. The officers ate the same meal at six o'clock.

27

In the officer's mess things were altogether more luxurious, with individual cabins for each of the scientists to work and rest. However, the bunks were right next to the hull and I'm sorry to say my timbers froze right through. Sometimes they had to chip icicles off the bolts in the walls before they could go to bed! If the ice melted that meant a wet bunk.

A hammock nearer the galley was much warmer...and dry!

Doctor Koettlitz was our ship's surgeon and photographer. He made sure that the men stayed healthy and gave everyone a regular check up, constantly on the look out for signs of the dreaded scurvy. His sick bay was right next to the galley because that was the only warm place.

"DISCOVERY"

Ernest Shackleton wrote a monthly newspaper called 'The South Polar Times'. There was just one copy, passed around the crew, explaining all the latest finds, with news, poems, jokes, cartoons and illustrations by Dr Wilson.

THE
South Polar Times
APRIL • 1902

Day after day the wind piled snow around and on top of me. Brrr! My black hull was white now and my masts and rigging were frozen stiff. Mind you, I never complained. The men cleared my decks each morning using shovels and brushes.

But it wasn't always blizzard conditions. I liked the clear nights best when the moon shone on the twinkling snow and I watched the Aurora Australis flash her colours across the midnight sky. I think the dogs liked these nights too because they would throw back their heads and howl to the moon, waking most of the men!

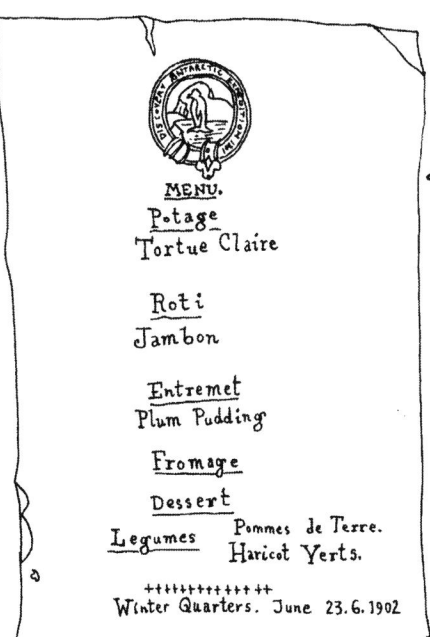

Christmas was celebrated on 23rd June which was mid-winter. The mess decks had paper decorations and the men were given small gifts that Captain Scott had kept hidden away. Christmas dinner was turtle soup, boiled ham with kidney beans and potatoes, followed by plum pudding with brandy sauce. There were cakes and sweets and the day ended with a concert.

Spring preparations

When the sun came up at the end of August the men got busy with sledging journeys. There was so much to discover out there! There were stores of food to be placed out on the ice for use as they returned from expeditions. I watched them come and go. Sometimes they took teams of dogs and sometimes the men pulled the sledges themselves. Often when they came back they looked terrible. They had frostbite, snow blindness and the dreaded scurvy. The dogs too were having a bad time. Many of them died out on the ice. Their food had gone bad and it was poisoning them. This made Captain Scott and the crew very sad.

In October Reginald Skelton returned with some exciting news. His team had seen and photographed an Emperor penguin rookery where the birds were huddled together, rearing their young chicks on the ice. This was an important discovery as previously it was thought they must go somewhere warmer to have babies. Dr Wilson was dying to get to Cape Crozier to have a look!

Farthest South expedition

On 2nd November 1902, Captain Scott left with Ernest Shackleton and Edward Wilson to go as far south as they could, maybe even to the south pole! Everyone cheered as they set off, but I felt nervous for them and the dangers they were walking towards. From my frozen harbour it was easy to imagine that the ice was the same all over. Smooth with a soft covering of snow. But I had learned from the men that this is not the case! There are huge deep cracks hidden in the ice that a man can't see until he falls in. Deadly crevasses of torn and twisted ice hundreds of metres deep. There are mountains to cross with glaciers moving ever so slowly to the coast. The ice can be smooth or ridged, sharp and jagged. **It sounded terrible.**

I can't tell you how relieved I was to spot three figures coming slowly back to me on 3rd February 1903. They were clearly exhausted, suffering from frostbite and scurvy, Shackelton was coughing up blood, but oh my, what tales they had to tell! They had reached their farthest south, not quite to the south pole, but they had discovered new land every day.

Dr Wilson had sketched everything even though he was badly affected by snow blindness. (Snow blindness is like having your eyes sunburnt. It is terribly painful, like having lots of sand in your eyes!) They had pulled their sledges by day and camped by night, often putting up their tent in blizzards with frostbitten hands and feet. Ouch! They had run low on food and looked very thin. Sadly not one of the dogs had survived.

Once on board they removed clothes that had not been off for 95 days and had a bath. Then they ate, and ate, and ate!

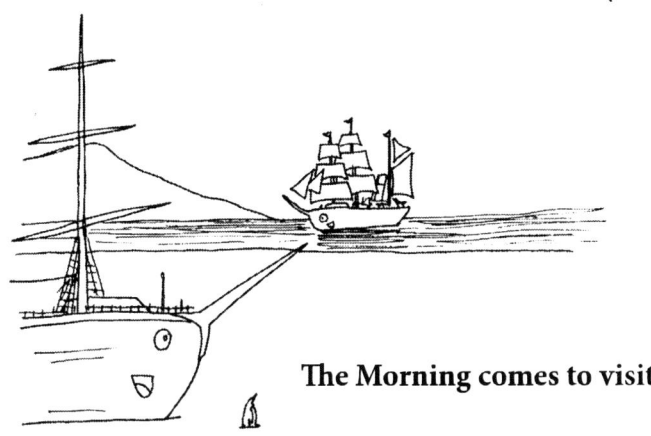

The Morning comes to visit

We had some exciting news for them too! Just a week before they returned our relief ship 'The Morning' had arrived and was berthed 16km away at the edge of the ice. They had picked up our message in the tin at Cape Crozier and come to find us. They brought fresh supplies of food for the men and coal for me. My crew mates were so happy to read letters from home, open parcels sent by their families and catch up on the news from the world we had left behind. It was great to have new company, and the men seemed to think the ice would break up and I would be free to sail once more. I felt a shiver of excitement run through my timbers when I heard this! It would be wonderful to sail home to Dundee! My engines were prepared, my sails shaken out, and I soon felt ship shape. Whoo hoo! All I needed now was for the ice to move out of the way! The summer sun was shining down and some ice broke allowing the Morning to get a tiny bit closer. I, however, remained stuck fast!

Shackleton goes home, we stay!

As the days became weeks and I still felt no movement under my hull, it became clear that Captain Scott was preparing to stay in Antarctica. The Morning had replenished our stocks, there were more discoveries to be made and the Captain said he trusted me to keep everyone safe for another year. To be honest I felt sad. I had been excited at the thought of racing through the waves again, freed from my icy prison. Ernest Shackleton was returning home on the Morning due to his poor health along with a few other sailors. I watched with sadness as he walked slowly away. I would miss Shacks, but I had a feeling he would be back to Antarctica before very long.

Orders were given to prepare me for winter, my sails were put away and my engine dismantled once again. The awning went back up over my deck.

Planning began again, journals were written up and Dr Wilson spent hours painting the sketches he had made the previous spring. Food for the sledging journeys was prepared and packed, skiis, tents and sleeping bags repaired. This year the Captain and his team would go west through the mountains while others would go south-west or back to the penguin rookery at Cape Crozier. But first the food depots had to be laid with flags on top so that they could be easily seen by hungry explorers.

Penguins make poor pets

Dr Wilson was very excited by the Emperor penguin rookery and he brought back eggs, frozen chicks and a live chick which he kept in the officer's wardroom. It may have looked like a cute and cuddly pet, but I can tell you, it was very noisy, demanding to be fed chewed up seal meat both day and night!

Exploration

Captain Scott and his team walked hundreds of kilometres through mountains, glaciers and plateaus. They collected lots of rocks and made measurements and maps of the new lands. They had several very close shaves, getting lost in blizzards, sliding down glaciers and falling into crevasses. Luckily they were tied together by ropes, but dangling four metres down inside an ice cave sounded rather terrifying to me.

Reginald Skelton our engineer and Hartley Ferrar the young geologist had been exploring too, and they had found a seam of coal in some rocks. When they examined the rock specimens they realised that Antarctica must have once been warm enough to grow trees and plants! From my frozen harbour, that was very, very hard to believe!

Stuck fast

Lieutenant Albert Armitage had been in charge while everyone was away exploring and thankfully he had put the remaining sailors to work, to set me free. I was so relieved. Then I saw that they were trying to cut the ice with saws! Were they mad?

There were over 32 kilometres of ice between me and the open sea! They had been sawing for ten days and nights when Captain Scott arrived. He ordered the men to stop when he saw how little progress they had made. I was getting very worried, I really didn't want to stay for another winter! I longed to feel the wind in my sails, the steam in my boilers once more! All I could do was pray for the weather and the tide to break up the ice **around my timbers.**

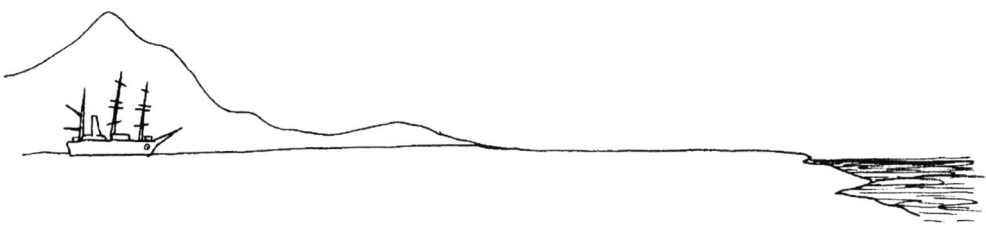

On 5th January 1904 the Morning returned to us along with the Terra Nova, an old friend of mine from Dundee! Just like me the Terra Nova had been built in Dundee. She was an old whaling ship under the command of Captain Henry McKay. These two ships had been sent to help us get home. Little did I know they had orders to abandon me if I wasn't free by the end of February! Captain McKay started blasting the ice with explosives and he kept at it for six weeks.

By 14th February 1904 Terra Nova and Morning had pushed their way alongside me for the first time. Yippee! Gradually I began to feel different!
Little by little I began to move as the ice broke and drifted away. All of a sudden my stern popped up as my keel was freed from the ice.

I cannot tell you how fantastic it felt to have water lapping round my sides. The men cheered and cheered, so happy that I, their beloved Discovery, would be taking them home.

Homeward bound

Antarctica didn't let me get away that easily however! On 17th February with my engines puffing away, the wind pushed me aground in a fierce storm. This time I thought my timbers were going to split as the waves picked me up and banged me down on the seabed. It was agony! After a few hours of this battle the wind finally dropped and I was able to get safely away. Thankfully my sturdy timbers had stood up to the worst of Antarctica yet again.

With Terra Nova and Morning we went back to New Zealand where we had the most wonderful welcome from our old friends. Then it was on to the Falkland Islands to finish the magnetic research, before sailing north to Britain.

A heroes welcome

We arrived in London on 15th September 1904 and what a sight for my tired timbers. Everyone had turned out to greet us, including our old shipmate Ernest Shackleton. I was very proud to bring my crew home to their loved ones, they were heroes every one. All who returned in me were awarded a special polar medal and Captain Scott was made a Commander of the Victorian Order by the King.

The expedition had brought more scientific findings from the mysterious, frozen south than ever before. People now knew about the geography, the weather, the ice, the sea, the land, the animals and the magnetic pole in that amazing place called Antarctica.

I had gone all that way, kept everyone safe and come back again.

Not bad for a little wooden ship from Dundee. Not bad at all.

Did you know?

Captain R.F. Scott
Captain Scott returned to Antarctica in 1910 on the Terra Nova. Sadly he died there in 1912 with Dr Wilson and three others. They had reached the South Pole several weeks after the Norwegian explorer Roald Amundsen. The weather was so bad they were stuck in their tent and they ran out of food and fuel. The next food depot was only 11 miles away, but they could not reach it.

Ernest Shackleton
Ernest Shackleton returned to Antarctica in 1907, 1914 and 1922 as captain on his own voyages. In 1914 his ship the Endurance was crushed by the ice and sank. Shackleton bravely took his men over the ice and sea to an uninhabited island and then set off to get help in a tiny boat. After a terrible struggle he managed to return and save all the men.

Edward Wilson
Edward Wilson had always loved nature, animals and drawing. He was a wonderful self-taught artist as well as a doctor. Captain Scott persuaded Edward to return to Antarctica on the Terra Nova in 1910. Sadly he died beside Captain Scott on their return from the South Pole in March 1912.

Tom Crean
Tom Crean went back to Antarctica with Shackleton and Captain Scott and had many adventures and close shaves! He saved the lives of several explorers with his strength and determination. He retired to Annascaul in Ireland where he opened the South Pole Inn.

Penguins
There are seventeen different species of penguin from the mighty Emperor to the little Blue penguin and they all live in the southern hemisphere. Although they can't fly they can swim very fast. The ones who live on Antarctica are : Emperor, King, Gentoo, Chinstrap, Rockhopper, Adelie and Macaroni. The others live in places such as Australia, S. Africa, S. America and the Galapagos Islands.

Visit me in Dundee
I am happy to say I came home to Dundee when I retired in 1986 and you can come and visit me. I have a brilliant 5 star visitor centre where you can find out more about Captain Scott's voyage and all the other adventures I had later on. Best of all, you can come aboard and see for yourself just how special I am. I love visitors!